THE WORK OF
Stephen Harvard
A LIFE IN LETTERS

Catalogue by David P. Becker

HARVARD COLLEGE LIBRARY · THE HOUGHTON LIBRARY

Department of Printing and Graphic Arts

CAMBRIDGE · MASSACHUSETTS · 1990

Production of the catalogue has been generously supported by Roderick Stinehour and the staff of Meriden-Stinehour Press in memory of their late colleague. The publication has been further supported and encouraged by many individuals and companies including: The Bulfinch Press of Little, Brown and Co., The Shagbark Press, Acme Bookbinding, Lance Hidy, Greg Heins, Tony King, John Stinehour, as well as other friends and admirers of Stephen Harvard. Additional support for the exhibition has come from the Society of Printers, Boston, of which Stephen Harvard was a member.

The photographs that appear in these pages are by Stephen & Paula Harvard and are from their personal files, with the following exceptions: Lance Hidy, pp. 2, 18 center, and 47 top and lower left; Ann Stewart, p. 63

Title page calligraphy by Christopher Stinehour

Catalogue copyright © 1990 by the President and Fellows of Harvard College

Selections from the writings and drawings
of Stephen Harvard copyright © 1990 by Paula Harvard

Adobe Illustrator is a trademark of Adobe Systems, Inc.
registered in the United States

ISBN 0-914630-04-0
LIBRARY OF CONGRESS CATALOG CARD NUMBER
90-080300

Catalogue published in conjunction with *The Work of Stephen Harvard*,
an exhibition held at the Houghton Library
23 April – 31 May 1990

Contents

Foreword   7

Introduction   9

Acknowledgments   11

Paragraphs on Life and Letters by Stephen Harvard   13

Exhibition Checklist   33
    SH AS DESIGNER
       Books   33
       Invitations, Posters, Broadsides   37
       Decorated Papers and Devices   40
       Type Designs   44
    SH AS STONECUTTER   46
    SH AS AUTHOR   48
    SH AS DRAFTSMAN AND ILLUSTRATOR   49

Published Writings   57

Catalogue of Inscriptional Stonework   59

Foreword

The houghton library has long cherished its close relationship with Stephen Harvard, which began when he was an undergraduate at Dartmouth. He frequently visited the Department of Printing and Graphic Arts, where his interest in the world of letters (what he later called the "material of literacy") was encouraged by Philip Hofer. Within a few years he was commissioned to design catalogues for us; later we were able to assemble a strong representation of his calligraphy, design, and printing in our collection; today we are privileged to mount an exhibition of his work and to publish this accompanying catalogue.

The artist who reveals himself in the words and images selected by David Becker was an extraordinary person: totally devoted to the graphic arts ("the art of the grid") but able to see them in a remarkably fresh and broad context. Stephen Harvard thought carefully about the future of the letters he created and the books he designed; realizing that they would inevitably enter the marketplace, he nevertheless wanted them to retain as much of the integrity of their creation as they could. He delighted in subtle variety—to adapt his own words—and it was a powerful and subtle mind indeed that could articulate the relationship between the work of his hand and the social and environmental issues that continue to haunt his generation.

We are able to explore the world of Stephen Harvard through the generosity of those who have lent examples of his work to this exhibition. We are particularly grateful to Roderick Stinehour, and to Paula Harvard and the members of her family, for enabling us to reveal this brilliant young artist's work as fully as possible.

Richard Wendorf
Librarian

Introduction

Stephen Harvard was the consummate craftsman: poised, assured, in total command of his materials. With a sure sense of form that invested his work with a distinctive artistry, he chose to see himself as a craftsman, gaining strength from the directness and honesty of this conception. In a short career he accomplished much, touched many, and left a significant body of work.

Born in Rochester, Minnesota in 1948, Stephen grew up in Connecticut, where his first interest was natural history, an awareness that trained his eye in careful observation and developed into an abiding understanding of nature and a closeness to the earth. At the same time, his talent and interest in the arts were developing. Along with his boyhood museum of natural history in the basement came the self-taught practice of calligraphy, a correspondence course in cartooning, and courses in etching and oil painting. Entering Dartmouth in 1966 with these developing skills, he was fortunate to become a student of Ray Nash, whose legendary courses in book design, printing, and printmaking focussed Stephen's gifts toward the area in which he was to perform so brilliantly. The unique legacy of Professor Nash was recalled by this young pupil some years later (see p. 13): "Ray Nash's students were apt to get more than they bargained for. They came for instruction but left, as likely as not, with a way of life." Tucked away in the basement of the Baker Library, under the auspices of the Department of Art at Dartmouth, Nash's courses preserved the studio/workshop tradition. He opened eyes, instructed hands, and taught the inseparable relation of materials and tools to design and expression.

Stephen's academic credentials were demonstrated in his election to Phi Beta Kappa, and before his graduation in 1970, he had spent a year on fellowship abroad, researching the collections of the Plantin-Moretus Museum in Antwerp, studying punchcutting and engraving with Sem Hartz in Haarlem, and stone cutting with Will Carter in Cambridge.

From this productive year came his first book, *Ornamental Initials: The Woodcut Initials of Christopher Plantin* (eventually published in 1974) and his realization that letters and graphic design would be his career. He then spent a year as a stonecutter at the John Stevens Shop in Newport. After performing alternate service as a conscientious objector, in 1973 he joined the Stinehour Press in Lunenburg, Vermont, where he had been a printer's devil as an undergraduate. Now he was book designer, illustrator, and calligrapher, and in 1983 he became corporate vice-president of the Meriden-Stinehour Press.

(The Stinehour Press and Meriden Gravure Company had joined forces and names in 1977.) In addition to the demands of his profession, and closely related to them, Stephen was always working with letters, cutting stone inscriptions, inscribing calligraphic ones, combining typographic and calligraphic elements. While he was perfecting his mastery of the most traditional of ancient crafts in inscriptional stone lettering, he was also designing alphabets for digital type. He was challenged by the fast growing and still fluid computer technology, understanding that such technology exists to serve and eager to use it in his search for form. And always he was drawing and writing, creating a world of pictures and words.

In the daily exercise of his profession, for which he received numerous awards, Stephen touched many lives, teaching us and sharing his gifts with us. His friends at the Houghton Library had worked with him for years on special projects, and he had chosen to form for us a collection of proofs of his printed calligraphy. It was always a proud day when we secured his participation in a publication, and an unfailing pleasure and challenge to work with him. It was a black day when we lost him. Because we want to record some of his achievements and to share something of what he gave and meant to us and to so many, we have been planning this exhibition and preparing the catalogue for the past year. It includes but a small portion of his output, representing the area in which we knew him best. Less than two years have elapsed since his death, and more exhibitions will be devoted to him in years to come. Included here are letter design, book design, inscriptions, and some of his own writings. David Becker's catalogue, with a checklist of the exhibition, also presents Stephen in his own words, which form a portrait of the artist, still a young man. In these pages (p. 19), he speaks of the perfectionism of the lettering craftsman and the "crystal-clear" alphabet in his mind. For him, this ideal alphabet of the mind existed to serve as a vehicle for literature, to convey a message that was essential to give meaning to the letterforms. This wholeness of approach animated all his work, relating each area to others and binding the whole together. For Stephen, nature and letters and literature were part of a mythic whole that animated his life and work.

Eleanor M. Garvey
Philip Hofer Curator of Printing and Graphic Arts
January 1990

Acknowledgments

IN WRITING OF HIS MENTOR Ray Nash, Stephen Harvard once declared that his life could not "be confined to the printed page." The same feeling strikes this writer in reflecting upon Stephen's own life. Despite a curtailed career, Stephen left a very large body of work indeed, and I have never been faced with as difficult a process in selecting such a relatively small group of objects. The present exhibition consists of merely a sampling, which I hope is representative of Stephen's gifts and hard-won achievements in so many areas of artistic endeavor. Because the work in book design and lettering has been emphasized, space limitations have regrettably restricted the inclusion of many of Stephen's drawings and illustrations, of which there could be an entire exhibition in themselves. Similarly, it was most difficult to include only two of Stephen's prose pieces in the exhibition and a small number of others in the catalogue, chosen from over a hundred finished pieces in his files.

It is my privilege to have had three of my own publications designed by Stephen, and I am privileged to have been asked by Eleanor Garvey to assemble this exhibition. In carrying out my task, I have received all possible aid from Miss Garvey and her assistant curator, Nancy Finlay, and from their assistant Brenda Breed. Richard Wendorf, Roger Stoddard, and Dennis Marnon of the Houghton Librarian's office have enthusiastically supported this project. Custodians of Stephen's work at other libraries have been unfailingly helpful, including Philip Cronenwett and Edward Connery Lathem of the Dartmouth College Library; Gay Walker of the Arts of the Book Room, Yale University Library; Dale Roylance of the Graphic Arts Collection, Princeton University Library; Ruth Mortimer, Smith College Library; and David Farrell, University of California, Berkeley, General Library.

Stephen's legion of friends, professional colleagues, and admirers have eagerly shared their collections, letters, and recollections with me and encouraged the exhibition project. I wish especially to thank William Bentinck-Smith, Carol Blinn, Michael Burton, Carolyn Coman, Cope Cumpston, David Godine, Jonathan Greene, Lance Hidy, Sinclair Hitchings, Katy Homans, Gregg Hugo, Jerry Kelly, Sandra Kirshenbaum, Nancy Southworth, and Sumner Stone. Stephen's brother Andrew Harvard supplied some essential information; their parents Dr. and Mrs. Marvin Harvard have been most supportive and generous with information and photocopies of letters.

Roderick Stinehour and all at the Meriden-Stinehour Press have helped this project in every way possible. It has been a particular pleasure to work with Rocky and Christopher Kuntze on the concept and design of this publication. In addition, Eleanor White and Stephen Stinehour have aided my efforts in numerous ways.

I should say a word about my compilation of Stephen's words in the following "essay," which I have called "paragraphs on life and letters." As I read through Stephen's letters, files, and published writings, I was continually struck by his eloquence and carefully considered thoughts as he committed them to paper. Rather than attempting to compose an expository essay describing or (worse) explaining Stephen's work, I thought it would be appropriate to let him speak for himself—necessarily in a group of fragments, but perhaps giving an idea of his own voice. The responsibility is mine in the choice of quotations; my editing of these pieces has been minimal, extending only to a few elisions, as indicated, in order to smooth an occasional passage, and to corrections of Stephen's sometimes eccentric spelling.

My greatest debt is to Paula Harvard, whose cooperation, hospitality, and encouragement have been vital to my completion of this project. She has been totally generous in her support, and I would like to dedicate my work to her, and to Shelagh and Kate Harvard.

David P. Becker
Curator of the exhibition

Paragraphs on Life and Letters by Stephen Harvard

Beginnings

I was born in Minnesota, 1948, and grew up in Connecticut, where my time was chiefly spent on an amorphous collection of local shells, fossils and insects, although even these vast fields were cheerfully expanded to include just about anything in the natural world when, say, a frog with five legs turned up in the woods across the street. Beyond this, I enjoyed drawing and cutting woodblocks, and, when the facilities were available, etching and letterpress printing. By the time I got to Dartmouth College I had realized that most of my interests were related to the arts of the book.[1]

*   *   *

Ray Nash's students were apt to get more than they bargained for. They came for instruction but left, as likely as not, with a way of life. That was his greatest strength: the vision to disclose a kind of work so rich and vital as to transcend a mere profession—a kind of work that was a way of living in the world; a way of making, rather than consuming, culture. . . .

He taught with tools and objects, never slides. Rembrandt etchings, Dürer engravings, Aldine incunabula, wood blocks from Bewick's hand, all came to the table to be touched, examined, talked about. He taught with presses, ink, and paper. He taught with friends, and with the world at large. A chance remark about Van Krimpen or Garamond might lead to a winter at Enschedé, a year on the Vrijdagmarkt, or both. . . .[2]

The success of his students in the workaday world certainly had roots in his realistic approach to printing. His workshop was no ivory tower. "I'm having trouble with this type (or ink, or press)," a student might say—but only once. The rejoinder was, "If trouble bothers you, you're in the wrong place."[3]

x   x   x

The most useful book in the reserve shelf for me this term has been Moxon's *Mechanick Exercises* on printing because of a new interest in hand presses and in punchcutting. If not the most useful, then perhaps the most beautiful and often-perused (and so, possibly the most useful after all) is Stanley Morison's collection of beautiful title pages.[4]

* * *

In 1968 I was a graphic artist learning to be a book designer. My taste and inclination was to the contemporary movements, as it should have been. But my study of history took me to the Plantin-Moretus Museum, and there my modernist theories received a staggering challenge. There, I found ancient letterforms more simple and direct and beautiful than those of my own generation. And there, for the first time, I realized that letters are ultimately hand-made objects, formed according to the materials and uses at hand, by the skill and sensibility of the craftsman. And so it was as a craftsman that I fell in love with letters, with the material of literacy—as a potter may love his clay or the carpenter his wood.[5]

* * *

The [Plantin-Moretus] Museum is beautiful, as is Antwerp itself—a snug Brueghelesque town fitted around a gothic cathedral. I will live in the old section, all narrow alleyways. . . . The natives are friendly, & like the same music I do.[6]

* * *

For all I've got here, I do miss being in New England in the fall. But it's worth the sacrifice. I see every day what a special time this is. The pressure-gauge has been released: I have time to think before I act, & I discover I do in fact have things on my mind, things I care about. I've been quite literally in a full time rat-race since early in H[opkins] G[rammar] S[chool]—summers included, as they were all part of the college panic. Now, magically removed from the whole system, I see things clearly: what I've lost and gained, what's for sale, and who's to pay. This breath of air is an extra I hadn't planned on, for which I'm very grateful. I've taken on a study of the 16th-century ornamental initials at the museum, which topic has been avoided by type experts who consider these to be woodcut illustrations, and by the woodcut people because they're typographical—leaving the field wide open for me. . . .[7]

* * *

I'm studying engraving under the hand of [a] wonderfully helpful man, the last of his trade. I work [at Enschedé en Zonen, Haarlem] where one of my heroes worked—Jan van Krimpen, perhaps the greatest type designer of this century. My host, Sem Hartz, is a stamp designer and a truly fine craftsman who constructs his own shotguns, making each part and engraving the metalwork. He's full of fascinating stories.[8]

✶   ✶   ✶

I'm afraid I've gotten to the stage where I'm sophisticated about the technicalities of old Books & Prints—15th–18th century—so that I can tell the good & genuine from the ordinary. . . . My collector's instinct is slowly but irrevocably beginning to stir, but this time I'll need a foundation grant to satisfy it. Art books are bad enough. I was better off when all I needed for satisfying that desire was a good stretch of woodland.[9]

✶   ✶   ✶

Everything's o.k.; I'm having a fine rest from Dartmouth's bureaucracy. Did you see my picture in the paper? I was put onto the first flight of Pan Am's hideous new Boeing 747, and was much photographed & interviewed. Most of the other passengers had booked 2 years in advance. . . .[10]

✶   ✶   ✶

Feder und Stichel [by Hermann Zapf] still provokes in me the same astonishment and excitement that it did when I first lovingly turned the pages of the proprietor's copy at Museum Books in New York in my student days. I would often go to that shop just to see and touch these two books. If someone had told me then that I would one day own a copy of *F&S* with a kind inscription from its author, I would not have believed him.[11]

✶   ✶   ✶

I have been active in this field since, as an undergraduate at Dartmouth, I studied with Prof. Nash and worked as a printer's devil for the Stinehour Press. In 1968 I went to Antwerp where I wrote a monograph on the Ornamental Initials of Christopher Plantin, to be published this year; I also spent several months in Haarlem, learning punchcutting with Sem Hartz and Mr. Hendrik Droste. When Will Carter came to Dartmouth as visiting artist, I was able to learn lettercutting in stone and wood, and Reynolds Stone, in his brief stay as lecturer, helped me with my interest in engraving calligraphy and illustrations on boxwood.

After leaving Hanover, I worked for a year as a lettercutter at the John Stevens Shop. For the past two years I have worked independently as a calligrapher, illustrator & stonecutter. My wife and I are now planning a move to New Hampshire, where I plan to settle permanently and pursue these crafts.[12]

✶   ✶   ✶

ORNAMENTAL INITIALS

THE WOODCUT INITIALS
OF CHRISTOPHER PLANTIN
A COMPLETE CATALOGUE BY
STEPHEN HARVARD

THE AMERICAN FRIENDS OF
THE PLANTIN-MORETUS MUSEUM
NEW YORK · MCMLXXIV

I would be happy to work at the [Stinehour] Press, if you could make use of my current professional fields of Design, Calligraphy, engraving, and illustration. A composing room job would of course be enjoyable, but it would seem too much of [a] sidetrack at this point after the time I've invested in those other areas and the satisfaction they give me. This is a subject worth pursuing.[13]

* * *

[Embarking on a catalogue, never finished, of Christopher Plantin's botanical woodcuts] There are 4000 blocks represented, nearly all in good condition, all beautiful. I am uplifted, not dismayed, by the quantity, because I delight in these images in the same way I delight in letterforms combined and recombined. I'm sure the same part of the mind's eye is at work here. In any case I'm in my proper element here—books, woodcuts, and natural history.[14]

* * *

[On a visit to Ray Nash several years after studying with him:] It was good to be there with him once again, talking shop about the roman majuscules—good to have come all that way into his world of Making Things; good to have found the colleagues and the friends his teaching led me to; good to hold the tools by second nature that he first directed to my hands. . . . Sometimes it all seems one long Making, letter after letter—a work transmitted to the hands of students, and their students; a great work unaffected by his passing; a work sustained into the future by his careful life.[15]

* * *

If you can add to this [advice] a *very strong* self-motivation, and a passion (or at least a slow boil) for making everything around you more beautiful, more useful, and more humane—then you'll be a very good designer indeed.[16]

On Letters and Other Matters

Why letters? They are useful, and like all useful things, subject to being made better or worse, graceful or ungainly, deft or inept. In short, they are susceptible to the craftsperson's skill like cups and cloth and cabinets.[17]

* * *

The lettering craftsman is apt to be a perfectionist—he is likely to have a crystal clear alphabet somewhere in his mind; a perfect, proportionate set of images that shine with pythagorean light. All of his work in the real world of ink, paper, copper, steel and stone will be an attempt, with varying degrees of success, to approach the ideal unseen letterforms. He is a craftsman who shares something with the artist as well as the mathematician; it is his trade as well as his joy to weigh form and proportion in his mind.

Of all the tasks that the lettering craftsman is likely to be asked to perform, the formal inscription is the one which will probably give him the nearest approach to realizing the ideal letterforms. That is, his other work—calligraphic manuscripts, punchcutting and type design, or whatever—has inherent limitations that inscriptional work does not. Each form has its own delights: but the delight of the inscription is that it usually provides the space, scale and material for the most nearly perfect letterforms that the craftsman can make. One who has come to truly love letters, will love inscriptions.[18]

* * *

The love of the literary content of the printed thing is the *sine qua non* of good work. Designing with a worthless text is like multiplying by zero: no matter how much you bring to the job, the result is always zero. We love literature and seek to enhance it with clear and sensible typography. We can aid the book but we can never elevate it.[19]

* * *

We are surely agreed that content is of overriding importance: Suaviter in Modo / FORTITER IN RE: Grace in style, strength in content . . . it makes all the difference to me whether my book or text is about a silverpolish manufacturer or a master silversmith. (Both jobs have come to me here.) I suppose the reason I know so little about advertising, and in fact the reason why I never went to school (graduate school) in graphics is a suspicion that these paths would lead away from, not toward, worthwhile content.[20]

* * *

If I were to say which among the various kinds of lettering provides the deepest satisfaction, I would quickly single out type design. Type design does not allow the freedom of calligraphy; the constraints imposed by typesetting machines are necessarily Procrustean. Nor does it result in anything as impressive as lettering carved in stone, the one medium alone in which roman capitals can be brought near to perfection. And yet printing types have a beauty and a power far beyond those other processes. A line of calligraphy is complete, but the letters of a typeface are charged with a tremendous kinetic energy.

Type design is a rather esoteric field for most educated people. Type designers are the nuclear physicists of the book world, dealing in elementary particles: the individual units from which pages and poems are composed.[21]

* * *

Type design in the punchcutting days had some parallels with sculpture—one person conceiving and executing the idea in three dimensions, altering the concept as he progressed. In this century it became more like architecture, with a designer more or less removed from the actual making, collaborating with skilled draughtspeople, engineers, and businessmen. If there is a conspicuous feature among the many new aspects of the craft, it is that now the older comparison obtains—that of the type-maker as designer and craftsman.[22]

*   *   *

It will be helpful to recognize 3 principles in analysing type forms.

    (1) The Framework – the basic stick shapes; Trajan, Aldine, carolingian—archetypes established through usage (not from Sinai) that may be ignored at peril.

    (2) Modules – the set of similar or repeatable shapes that give a type its dress.

    (3) Emerson's principle – foolish consistency – and the Whim corollary. That's what we see from the best designers: a rule established, obeyed nine times and ignored the tenth.

The graphic arts are the art of the grid, but in looking for excellence I look not for the closest adherence to the grid but the most intelligent deviation from it.[23]

*   *   *

Since their development and perfection during the imperial age, the roman capitals, displayed here, have been a test and a touchstone for the scribes of every generation. A test, because each new age requires the old forms to be reshaped to its own urgent requirements; and a touchstone, because no calligrapher, however deft, can leave the models far behind and hope to be intelligible. The large alphabet on this page is hand-lettered; it reveals the scribe's admiration for the vigorous reinterpretation of the roman capitals that took place in Italy during the sixteenth century among punchcutters, calligraphers, and designers of monumental inscriptions.[24]

*   *   *

Almost alone among his contemporaries, [Giovan Francesco Cresci] cut through the fond myth that Roman majuscules were beautiful due to some secret Vitruvian geometry, lost since the fall of the Caesars. He saw (correctly, in the best modern view, although the constructionist heresy still lingers) that good roman capitals can be made only by the trained hand and eye, not by compasses, straight-edge and grid.[25]

*   *   *

The dream of a workable, simple constructed roman alphabet is like the dream of perpetual motion. The patron of Vitruvian letter analysis must surely be Saint Lawrence, for he, too, was tortured on a grid.[26]

*   *   *

The current revolution has brought such wonders as the invisible, intangible typefont, and the typesetting machine with no moving parts. As it happens, the potential of these new digital typesetters to produce good work is excellent. Whether or not this potential is realized depends on which of two conditions in the trade prevails. The first is characterized by a word not yet in the O.E.D.—a neologism, perhaps not a good one, but one that stands for a good idea. The word is ergonomics: the science of adapting machines to the needs of people, rather than the other way round. The technical skill now exists to make electronic typesetting perfectly suited to the needs of intelligent, educated readers. Opposed to this is a word of excellent lineage, a word with O.E.D. citations back to Shakespeare: *bloodymindedness*. For it is corporate bloodymindedness to allot decisions to marketing people that are rightly the province of professional typographers.[27]

The Society of Printers

will meet on Wednesday, April 2, 1980, at the Club of Odd Volumes, 77 Mount Vernon Street Social Hour: 5:30 to 6:30 PM   Dinner: 6:30 PM Reservations must be received by the secretary, Mrs. Patricia Thoma, by Friday, March 28, 1980, or call 725–5634. All reservations not honored will be invoiced.

OFFICERS: James W. Hamilton, *President*; Stephen P. Snyder, *Vice-President*; Patricia A. Thoma, *Secretary*; Duncan Todd, *Treasurer*; Stephen Pekich, *Auditor*. COUNCIL: Richard C. Bartlett, Roy H. Brown, John Chipman, David Ford

Stephen Harvard

book designer, type designer, and calligrapher, will present an illustrated talk, *Living by Letters*. He will survey his current work as a lettering artist for media as diverse as carved stone and electronic photocomposition.

✳   ✳   ✳

These are curious times: everyone knows that we need typefaces to match the newest machines, but progress on the hardware end is so rapid (with no end in sight) that a designer is never on firm ground. The principles of a good type are constant, but the consummation is in the details—and the hardware controls, distorts, and dictates the details. We need a Model T or VW Bug typesetter; something that can remain a standard long enough for the good workers (that every generation supplies in good measure) to catch up with it.[28]

✳   ✳   ✳

How many typefaces do we need? Do we need another typeface? The answer is not an absolute—it depends on who's asking. Do we need any more varieties of Grey Riesling, or another bluegrass tune or contradance figure? If you can't tell the difference between the ones we already have, then the sensible answer for you is *no*. But if you delight in subtle variety, in incremental change, in nuance, in gesture, then you will welcome new wine and new song.[29]

✳   ✳   ✳

[Commenting on his own experiments on the computer interpolating type forms] This is pretty exciting stuff for me. As I've said to anyone who'll sit still, the lack of proportional sizes is the major scandal of the current type scene. If Adobe can build this kind of interpolation into output devices so that it happens on the fly with no pain or expertise extracted from the operator, then a major victory will have been won. Onward! You and your crew [at Adobe Systems] are fighting the good fight. These things *matter*![30]

✳   ✳   ✳

The main thing is that a page set in a new type not look like the last scene in Macbeth—a field of dead. Whatever the philosophy or esthetic rules, only a type lively enough to engage the eye will be easy to read.[31]

✳   ✳   ✳

The use of calligraphy and handlettering with printing types has been a recurring minor theme in books which I have designed during recent years. . . . 'Minor' is the proper adjective, since it is the making of purely typographic books, and of typographic books illustrated with photographs, that has involved the majority of my time and attention, so far as book design is concerned.

In contrast to this, I also work as a calligrapher and inscriptional stonecutter—trades which antedate (and may survive) the typographic book. In general, these two fields—calligraphy and typography—are necessarily kept separate, so it is a particular pleasure when circumstances call for the use of handlettering in printed books.

. . . . I have engraved and cut letters on a variety of materials with keen and continuing pleasure, and I delight in fine incised lettering of all historical periods. But on the other hand, my experience with the camera is that it is a subtle and valuable tool, capable of returning infinite rewards for judicious use. Wherever light, lens, and film enter the printing process, there also goes calligraphy with ease and grace.

In the case of lettering for reproduction, it is the printed piece that is the goal, the end. Printed lettering is not an inferior approximation of a remote "original"—it is itself the original. The drawing on paper is only one of several stages in its development, like the engraver's layout or the punchcutter's pattern.[32]

✽   ✽   ✽

What we must avoid in book design is the creation of a typographic Brasilia—an enterprise planned according to the most advanced theories, but inaccessible and undernourishing to the spirit. Books and cities are not art—they are tools for living. Fine art can do as it pleases; but typography, that humble implement, must strive to satisfy the intelligence rather than the intelligentsia.[33]

✽   ✽   ✽

The problem of the cover photograph—is it to be an image that has historical or other nonvisual importance, or is it to have great visual significance. If the publisher cannot understand the difference between these two categories, and see the importance of considering the latter, then the battle will be uphill, if it is not already lost.

We can debate the purpose of the cover, but surely we can all agree that it is not to present scholarly information. My own view is that it must be a visual statement, and that it must, given marketing, be a poster for the book. But this can and must be done with taste, with consideration for the author and for the world at large. Let us not commit ourselves to thoughtful writing and careful editing and let the cover lie where it may fall. Tasteful appropriate jackets clothe even bestsellers, when the publisher sees fit. The rest of the design that one sees in bookshops—where does it come from? From that same . . . culture that spins out the fast food palace and the colonial television set.[34]

✽   ✽   ✽

Here, at last, is the finished rendering of the centennial emblem [for the Club of Odd Volumes]. I have considered, I think, all of the comments on the earlier sketch that you thoughtfully collected and sent to me. The ink ball is now somewhat smaller in relation to the book, and of a different shape. I am now something of an expert on the iconography of pre-seventeenth century inking rockers and I can say that this one is of average form: the pad appears, in old engravings, to be nearly flat or nearly spherical or anything in between. The handle length and form also varies. . . . I am sorry that something the size of a postage stamp has had so long a gestation.[35]

* * *

If craft printers see themselves as preservers of letterpress and all its attendant processes, then they will have as little influence on the shape of new letterforms as stamp collectors. If however they see themselves as small experimental outposts of the current trade practice, bringing to contemporary problems and current equipment the advantage of unpressured labor, flexibility, wide education, devotion to ideals—then their influence will be profound, as profound perhaps as Morris's.[36]

* * *

I may not know [what the] fine press movement may be, but I know what it is not—it is not made up of people who say "dynamite, baby."[37]

* * *

Drawing with a pen or pencil is great—it's always high resolution, always WYSIWYG [what you see is what you get], and the hardware and software are the best.[38]

* * *

To design—to work by design and not by chance or luck—is the printer's goal. To him, design is the bone and muscle, not the outward dressing, of the book.[39]

* * *

There is a notable imbalance to the law of supply and demand when it comes to culture. Take a quick count: in every generation, there are more people who consume culture than those who create it; there are more people involved in the pursuit of happiness than in its making.[40]

* * *

The Centennial Book

Number 77 Mount Vernon Street

Boston, Massachusetts

What is craftsmanship? A way of working, an attitude, a degree of attention to detail, a mastery of a field of information, experience. This has nothing to do with any particular technology—any set of tools—and it has nothing to do with esthetic theory.[41]

Meditations

Paula and I are busy (people come to the region and always wonder "what you do here"—*we* haven't had time to ask), but coping, and have faith that a double-duty July will lead to some relaxation in August.[42]

* * *

Since we left you at 7:00 AM that Saturday in Maine, life has been like falling out of a fully-laden canoe into a stretch of whitewater: the boat, the gear & the passengers all arrive at their destination, but at a speed much faster than intended, and in considerable disarray.[43]

* * *

My life away from the press is busy, with not much creative work at present, but as much family time as possible, some cycling, some work on the land and house. . . . I am unconnected to any grapevines at present—except the big grapevine of the natural world, which continues to bring me news of a kind, and year by year returns me to the great pleasures of my boyhood, when nature, not art, was my love. So that too may be a renaissance of sorts.[44]

* * *

I'm absolutely certain that we were meant to appreciate the details of the universe. The fact that the undersides of leaves are as miraculously constructed as the tops, the fact that the surface of a single berry is as splendid as a sunrise sky, the fact that a roadside bush is fine as a redwood—these facts convince me that we are designed to be aware of everything: not just the flowers but the roots; not just the stars but the intricate feldspar flecks across a chip of granite. On a very important level these things are equally alive and important. . . .

I have never had any luck in my life making headway in formal religions (although I respect and even envy those who do, and although I continue to read texts of all religions) but I have at least been able to come to this one certainty: that we must *notice* the endlessly complex and beautiful world, and that we must *respond* to it, with praise, with art, with changes to our lives and culture.⁴⁵

*   *   *

What, in the universe, is small? Complaints and monuments.⁴⁶

*   *   *

The daring of breaking tradition on the spur of the moment, and the happy results, carry a quiet lesson for me: there is probably something worthwhile whichever way you step—as long as you do take a step in *some* direction.⁴⁷

*   *   *

It was a perfect day for a beginning. Crowberry bushes scrawled the edges of the cliff. Sanskrit juniper inscribed the peak. The broad dark sky unrolled above like parchment waiting for illumination.⁴⁸

*   *   *

Words, assemble! Gather into feather, wing, and bone. Words, be talon and crest and sparkling eye. Assemble, words, into the bright bird of imagination.⁴⁹

*   *   *

Calligrapher, turning your broad-edged pen to each serif and swash, can you remember the egg or the seed of thought that impels you to write? Was it a woman's clear quiet eye and half-turned head seen in the morning years ago? An empty farmhouse in the moonlight? Or some wild hill-thing, gray and rising into consciousness—an ancient maple tree against the sky, a river-colored hawk at dawn?⁵⁰

*   *   *

Gather in the generous decades as they come. Take peace from your life of useful work. Take pleasure in your thriving dooryard flowers. Take love, tonight, from your friends around this table. And harvest strength from the furrowed, star-sown pasture of the August sky.⁵¹

*   *   *

Even you will live in a time of miracles. Even you will have some necessary work to do. There will be a sheaf of paper and good black ink; there will be a jar of chinese brushes on the window sill. Even at this late date a new song will be useful. Even the flow of fresh calligraphy will help; even the careful binding of a book; even a well-made loaf of bread. Who can say? Even the smallest drawing of a cricket could serve some unimagined purpose to the troubled spirit of your age.[52]

* * *

WHAT THE WINE GLASS SAID

I had a fiery education. Inside my incandescent early world I flowed with liquid possibility. Youth, for me, was heat and flux, and I myself was fluid light. Alert, I took whatever came, and so became informed. I drew a single inhalation and expanded the globe. But my first breath became my last, and that brief youthful inclination froze into my only shape.

Later, I was purposeful and cold. Brittle, upstanding, transparent, empty: my role was to contain. I took the color of my work, no longer having color of my own. It was my fate to serve; it was my fate to be admired.

But I still had one deep idea. The years went by. I saw my chance. I made a necessary leap. In one swift arc of concentration I reclaimed my old prerogative of form. Your plans for me, it seems, were flawed. Now look: I am a hundred crystal prisms, splashing joyous fluent color on your wall.[53]

* * *

I come to you empty from too much travel. I come to you empty from too much talk. I come to you hollow and dry as a common reed—but a reed that only lacks the saving flow of words to be a broad-edged pen. Make me your pen, tall language of the wind. Make me your pen, great lexicon of stars and juniper and ice.[54]

* * *

ORIGIN

One of the places where the world begins is under this abandoned shed. Out here the universe looks like a mother fox. The universe is lithe and wary, graceful, tired, underfed, and serious. Her four brown kits play in the sun, brash as the first four foxes in the world, optimistic as the dawn. The universe, their mother, watches quietly while her work unfolds.

One of the places where the world begins is in between these granite stones. This was a corner too tight for grazing cows, so now an old wild apple tree leans out across the shed. In middle-May the universe prepares to grow its tart green fruit that nobody will taste—unless, by chance, some solitary walker comes this way in August; someone schooled in the secret flavors of the world.

Welcome, friend, to the center of the universe. The world always begins wherever you stand. And now you stand in a northern hillfarm pasture, watching the universe renew itself. This is where the foxes and wild apples take their shape, here in the intricate meadow grass of May. The center of the universe is always here. One of the places where the world begins is now.[55]

NOTES

NOTE: I am most grateful for Paula Harvard's generous, unrestricted permission to quote from Stephen Harvard's published writings and unpublished manuscripts. My sources for manuscript material, especially letters, are indicated at the end of each endnote; I have noted if I have relied on photocopies. PH = Paula Harvard; MSP = Stephen Harvard's files at Meriden-Stinehour Press.

1. Draft of a letter to Dorothy Markinko, 1 Jan. 1973 [despite ms, which is dated 1972], concerning application to illustrate a children's book [PH].

2. "The Long Making," *Ray Nash and the Graphic Arts Workshop at Dartmouth College* (Edward Connery Lathem, ed.), Hanover, The Friends of the Dartmouth Library, 1987, pp. 69, 72.

3. Unpublished draft for Ray Nash obituary in *Proceedings of the American Antiquarian Society*, vol. 97, pt. 1 (1987) [MSP].

4. Written response to an examination question in Professor Nash's Art 41, Fall Term 1967 [Special Collections, Dartmouth College Library].

5. Manuscript notes for a lecture [n.d.; PH].

6. From two undated letters to parents during junior year abroad in Antwerp, Belgium, October 1968 [Dr. and Mrs. B. Marvin Harvard].

7. Letter to parents, "End of October," 1968, from Antwerp [Dr. and Mrs. Harvard].

8. Letter to parents, January 1969, from Haarlem, The Netherlands [Dr. and Mrs. Harvard].

9. Letter to parents, 6 Mar. 1969, from Antwerp [Dr. and Mrs. Harvard].

10. Letter to parents, 28 Jan. 1970, from Antwerp [Dr. and Mrs. Harvard].

11. Letter to Hermann Zapf, thanking him for the gift of two of his books, *Feder und Stichel* and *Manuale Typographicum*, 20 July 1987 [copy; PH].

12. Letter to Philip Hofer, 16 July 1973 [Department of Printing and Graphic Arts, The Houghton Library, Harvard University].

13. Draft of a letter to Roderick Stinehour, 9 Apr. 1973 [PH].

14. Letter to Ray Nash, 23 Dec. 1976 [Dartmouth College Library]. Stephen's manuscript draft [MSP] reads: "I delight in the subtle variations among plants as among letterforms."

15. "The Long Making," *Ray Nash and the Graphic Arts Workshop at Dartmouth College* (Edward Connery Lathem, ed.), Hanover, The Friends of the Dartmouth Library, 1987, pp. 72–73.

16. Letter to Maeve Cullinane, giving advice about becoming a designer, May 1988 [copy, MSP].

17. Manuscript lecture notes [n.d.; PH].

18. Manuscript lecture notes [n.d.; PH].

19. Manuscript lecture notes [n.d.; PH].

20. Letter to Lance Hidy [n.d., after 8 Mar. 1977; Lance Hidy].

21. Manuscript lecture notes [n.d.; PH].

22. Manuscript lecture notes [n.d.; PH].

23. Manuscript lecture notes [n.d.; PH].

24. *Alphabets of Grace—A Calendar of Letterforms & Type Designs* [month of June], Dobbs Ferry, Cahill & Company [1985]. The "handlettered" alphabet is of course Stephen's own, as rendered in letterpress.

25. Review of A. S. Osley, *Scribes and Sources: Handbook of the Chancery Hand in the Sixteenth Century*, in *Fine Print*, vol. 7, no. 1 (Jan. 1981), p. 28.

26. Manuscript lecture notes [n.d.; PH].

27. Excerpt from an outline of a lecture delivered to the Club of Odd Volumes, Boston, 1981, accompanying a letter to Peter Wick, 5 Mar. 1981 [Department of Printing and Graphic Arts, The Houghton Library, Harvard University].

28. Letter to Jerry Kelly, 27 Mar. 1987 [Jerry Kelly].

29. Manuscript lecture notes [n.d.; PH].

30. Letter to Sumner Stone, 29 Jan. 1988 [Sumner Stone].

31. Manuscript lecture notes [n.d.; PH].

32. "Calligraphy for the Typographic Book," *Fine Print*, vol. 3, no. 3 (July 1977), p. 49.

33. Manuscript lecture notes [n.d.; PH].

34. Manuscript lecture notes [n.d.; PH].

35. Letter to Peter A. Wick, 19 Mar. 1986 [copy, MSP]

36. Manuscript lecture notes [n.d.; PH].

37. Manuscript lecture notes [n.d.; PH].

38. Manuscript lecture notes [n.d.; PH].

39. *Vision & Revision—Introducing Meriden-Stinehour Incorporated*, Meriden and Lunenburg, 1979, caption under plate 5.

40. "A Toast in Absentia, 4 July 1988" [broadside printed by Meriden-Stinehour Press in honor of Sandra Kirshenbaum].

41. Manuscript lecture notes [n.d.; PH].

42. Letter to parents, 11 July 1986 [Dr. and Mrs. Harvard].

43. Letter to parents, 10 Sept. 1986 [Dr. and Mrs. Harvard].

44. Letter to Lance Hidy, 15 Oct. 1985 [Lance Hidy].

45. Letter to Christopher Burkett, 18 Dec. 1987 [copy, MSP].

46. From prose piece entitled "Teacher" [typescript, PH].

47. Letter to parents, 27 Dec. 1986 [Dr. and Mrs. Harvard].

48. From prose piece entitled "Clean Slate" [manuscript, PH].

49. From prose piece entitled "Avalanche" [manuscript, PH].

50. From prose piece entitled "Source" [typescript, PH].

51. From prose piece entitled "The Garden," privately printed for Paula Harvard's birthday, 26 Aug. 1986.

52. From prose piece entitled "The Smallest Drawing of a Cricket" [typescript, PH]. The complete piece was published with a small drawing of a cricket by SH in *Printing History 20*, vol. 10, no. 2 (1988), p. 3.

53. Typescript [PH].

54. From prose piece entitled "Again" [manuscript, PH].

55. Printed for the memorial gathering, Lancaster, New Hampshire, 1 Aug. 1988.

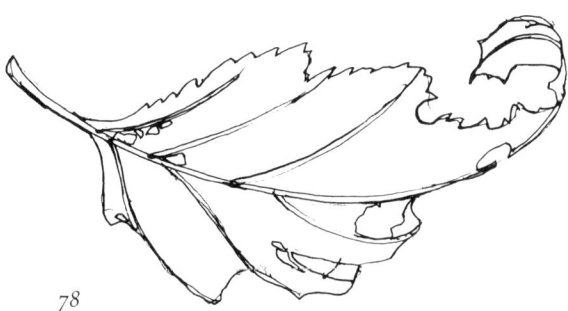

78

Exhibition Checklist

NOTES TO THE CHECKLIST: *Unless otherwise indicated, all material has been lent to the exhibition by Paula Harvard (manuscript and unpublished materials) and by Meriden-Stinehour Press (published works). Measurements are height before width.*

SH AS DESIGNER

Books

1

Major Acquisitions of The Pierpont Morgan Library 1924–1974

New York, The Pierpont Morgan Library, 1974
11¾ x 9 in.

A boxed set of four volumes: *Medieval & Renaissance Manuscripts, Early Printed Books, Drawings,* and *Autograph Letters & Manuscripts.* Winner of the Bronze Medal for Book Design at the 1975 Leipzig International Book Exhibition, "The Best Books in the World."

2

The Natural History of Carolina, Florida & the Bahama Islands, by Mark Catesby

Savannah, The Beehive Press, 1974
21¾ x 15½ in.

SH commented on his binding design: "The lettering was stamped with genuine gold from a one-piece handfinished die of ¼" brass alloy. The Roman letterforms were made with a square-cut, round-ferruled sable brush which dresses down to a sharp chisel edge. The brush forms the weighted elements of the letters in one pass as an edged pen would, but unlike a pen it can produce true serifs in easy, natural strokes—an accomplishment that no other writing implement can match." ("Calligraphy for the Typographic Book," *Fine Print*, vol. 3, no. 3 [1977], p. 52.)

3

200 Years of American Sculpture, ca. 1975

Brush, black ink, and gouache on laid paper
17¼ x 12¾ in.

Lent by David R. Godine Publisher, Inc.

Original hand lettering commissioned by Lance Hidy, was intended—but never used—for the binding of the exhibition catalogue published by the Whitney Museum of American Art and David R. Godine.

4

A Printer's Emblems

[Lunenburg, The Stinehour Press, 1976]
4¾ x 6 in.

SH wrote the texts accompanying his hand-lettered designs for the several mottoes. (Writings catalogue no. W2)

5

Images of Childhood—An Exhibition of Pictures and Objects from Nineteenth-Century New Bedford

New Bedford, Old Dartmouth Historical Society, 1976
11 x 8½ in.

6

William Morris and the Art of the Book

New York, The Pierpont Morgan Library, 1976
11¾ x 9 in.

Beyond the classic SH design of the text, the covers of this exhibition catalogue reveal his innovative use of a

THE LYRICAL POEMS OF

In the original French, & in the English versions by Algernon Charles Swinburne, Dante Gabriel Rossetti, William Ernest Henley, John Payne, and Léonie Adams; selected by Léonie Adams. With an introductory essay by Robert Louis Stevenson

THE LIMITED EDITIONS CLUB
NEW YORK · MCMLXXIX

THE GROLIER CLUB

1884 – 1984

ITS LIBRARY, EXHIBITIONS, & PUBLICATIONS

NEW YORK · 1984

Morris watermark design combined with a reproduction of a laid paper texture. SH designed a majority of the exhibition catalogues produced by the Morgan Library from the mid-1970s until 1988, particularly those for old master drawings.

7

Wash and Gouache—A Study of the Development of the Materials of Watercolor, by Marjorie B. Cohn

Cambridge, Center for Conservation and Technical Studies, Fogg Art Museum, 1977
8 x 10 in.
The cover and title lettering are by SH, and the cover design is reproduced from A.M. Perrot, *Manuel du coloriste* [Paris, 1834].

8

Plain & Elegant, Rich & Common— Documented New Hampshire Furniture 1750–1850

Concord, New Hampshire Historical Society, 1978
11 x 7 ½ in.

9

Twelve Centuries of Bookbinding, by Paul Needham

New York, The Pierpont Morgan Library, 1979
12 x 9 in.

10

The Lyrical Poems of François Villon, selected by Léonie Adams

New York, The Limited Editions Club, 1979
11 x 7 ¼ in.
The typography, calligraphy, decorative endleaves, and binding were all the design of SH.

11

Yosemite and the Range of Light, by Ansel Adams
Boston, New York Graphic Society, 1979
12 ¼ x 15 ¼ in.
SH lettered the titling, including the NYGS logo, for this influential book designed by Lance Hidy. SH also did the lettering for a striking series of large posters using Adams photographs (see No. 26).

12

Drawings for Book Illustration—The Hofer Collection, by David P. Becker

Cambridge, Department of Printing and Graphic Arts, The Houghton Library, Harvard University, 1980
8 ½ x 9 ½ in.

13

The Art of the French Illustrated Book, by Gordon N. Ray

New York, The Pierpont Morgan Library, 1982
12 x 9 ¼ in.

14

The Grolier Club 1884–1984

New York, The Grolier Club, 1984
11 x 8 ½ in.
The letters on the title and initial letters in the text are developed from the prototypes of SH's "Grolier" display type (see No. 46).

15

The Printer & the Pardoner, by Paul Needham
Washington, Library of Congress, 1986
11 x 8 ½ in.

16

In Spite of Everything, Yes, Ralph and Caroline Steiner, eds.

Albuquerque, University of New Mexico Press for the Hood Museum of Art, Dartmouth College, 1986
10½ x 9⅜ in.

17

The Age of Bruegel—Netherlandish Drawings of the Sixteenth Century

New York, The Pierpont Morgan Library, 1987
8½ x 10¼ in.

18

Legacies of Genius—A Celebration of Philadelphia Libraries—A Selection of Books, Manuscripts, and Works of Art, Edwin Wolf 2nd, ed.

Philadelphia, Philadelphia Area Consortium of Special Collections Libraries, 1988
11 x 8½ in.

Invitations, Posters, Broadsides

19

A History of the Photographic Book, 1977
Offset, 6¼ x 4½ in.
Announcement for a lecture by Lance Hidy at the Stinehour Press.

20

Hand Made Paper, 1977
Letterpress, 14¾ x 5½ in.
Announcement for a workshop by Walter Hamady at the Stinehour Press.

21

Inter Scientias Non Minima Est Typographica, 1977
Offset, 17 x 13 in.
Poster for a seminar in Graphic Design at the King Library Press, University of Kentucky. Participants were SH, John Dreyfus, Adrian Wilson, and Joyce Lancaster Wilson.

22

A B & C, 1980
Letterpress, 11 x 8½ in.
Announcement for a lecture by SH, "Living by Letters," at the Society of Printers, Boston.

23

The Adaptation of Ink Printing to the Photographic Image
Offset, 6¼ x 4½ in.
Announcement graphically illustrating the topic of a lecture by Richard Benson at the Meriden Gravure Company.

24

A Pearl
Graphite, ¼ in. diam. (image); 11 x 8½ in. (sheet)
Study for the above invitation.

25

The Craftsman Type Designer, 1981
Letterpress, 15¼ x 4½ in.
Announcement for a lecture by SH at the Club of Odd Volumes, Boston.

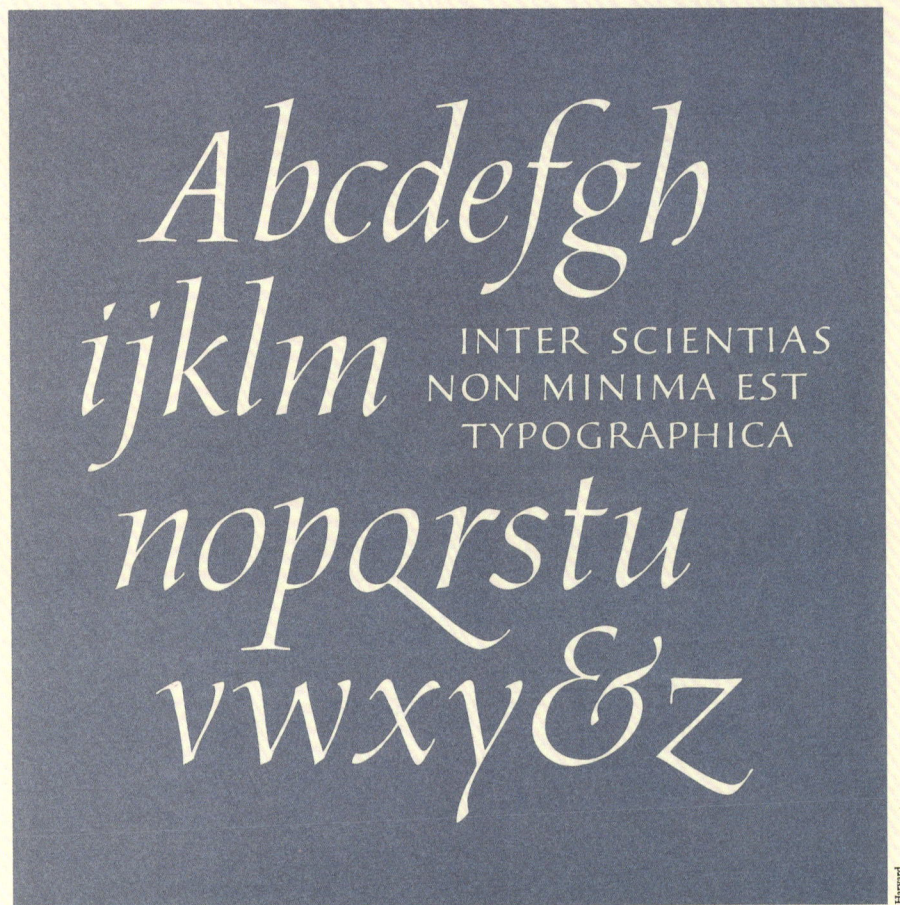

Seminar in Graphic Design at the King Library Press
University of Kentucky   28–31 October 1977

A fine print competition for printers in the Southeast, and four days of lectures, seminars, and demonstrations by:

JOHN DREYFUS, chairman, Printing Historical Society, and typographic advisor to Cambridge University Press

STEPHEN HARVARD, stonecutter, calligrapher, author, and designer at The Stinehour Press

ADRIAN WILSON, designer, historian, and proprietor of The Press in Tuscany Alley

JOYCE LANCASTER WILSON, educator, author, and illustrator of children's books

Sponsored by the University of Kentucky College of Library Science, Graduate Seminar Fund, King Library Press, and the Department of Art; the National Endowment for the Arts; and the Southern Federation of State Arts Agencies

27

26

Ansel Adams—The Print, 1984

Letterpress poster, 36 x 25 ½ in.

After the success of his display lettering for the 1979 *Yosemite and the Range of Light* (see No. 11), SH was commissioned to design a series of fifteen large posters utilizing photographs by Ansel Adams. The impression exhibited is one of a limited letterpress edition.

27

National Collegiate Book Arts, 1987

Offset, 19 ½ x 36 in.

"Perhaps the enclosed poster will interest you—if only as an example of how an excellent press crew refused to be defeated by a wholly unreasonable demand for solid coverage!" (Letter to Jerry Kelly, 19 Mar. 1987)

28

A Toast in Absentia, 4 July 1988

Letterpress broadside, 16 x 20 in.

With the numerous trials for the monogram and the innovative enlargement of the final graphite drawing, an insight can be gained into the lettering artist's working procedures. This work was printed as a birthday greeting for Sandra Kirshenbaum, publisher of *Fine Print*. (Writings catalogue no. W 17)

29

Sketches for SK / 50 Monogram, 1988

Graphite, 11 x 8 ½ in.
Studies for the above broadside.

30

Meriden-Stinehour Press, 1988

Offset poster, 33 ⅞ x 10 in.
A relatively colorful and free calligraphic design by SH, used for a New Year's greeting.

31

The Electronic Scriptorium: Two Cheers for Desktop Design, 1988

Offset, 11 x 8 ½ in.
Executed for a lecture given by SH to the Society of Printers, Boston, the display alphabet shown here was drawn on a computer screen; it was a current version of his "Grolier" face (see No. 46). This invitation was an example of artwork produced by SH without touching pen or brush to paper.

Decorated Papers and Devices

Among the less "glamorous" sides of book design are the individual decorative touches which can be such important additions to the ensemble. By his own count, SH designed over thirty individual logos for publishers, learned societies, and single books (including at least one used on a tie, for the Club of Odd Volumes, Boston). Although small in size, these commissions often involved considerable shaping and refining. SH indulged a freer side of his design sense in a considerable number of decorative papers used for endpapers or bindings, in which he varied a single small decoration in many combinations, sometimes drawing the elements himself, as in the Godine Chapbook cover (see No. 32).

32

Decorative Paper Design for Godine Poetry Chapbooks, 1978

Offset, 8 ¾ x 5 ¾ in. (individual binding)
This pattern was picked from a number of trial designs for decorative papers executed for the Third Godine Poetry Chapbook series, here seen on the cover of Gail Mazur, *Nightfire*, Boston, David R. Godine, 1978.

33

Two Sketches for Decorative Elements

Graphite, 4 x 4 in. each (image)
Preliminary sketches for the element used in the Godine Poetry Chapbook series (see No. 32, 34).

34

Four Trial Designs for Decorative Papers

Photostat, 5 ⅞ x 5 ⅝ in.

35

Individual Logos:

The Kentucky Review, 1979
The Club of Odd Volumes, ca. 1986
Proceedings of the American Antiquarian Society, 1987
Northern New Hampshire Foundation, ca. 1987

36

Bookplate for The Philip Hofer Collection, 1986

Offset, 2 ½ x 2 in.
Commissioned by The Houghton Library for the collection bequeathed by Philip Hofer in 1984. SH used the design for the cover of the 1988 exhibition catalogue of the Hofer Bequest. At this same time, he had been invited to submit designs for a more contemporary rendering of the Harvard Seal, and had experimented with many variations of the familiar logo utilizing "VE RI TAS" on three open books.

37

Device for the Princeton University Press, 1988

Graphite sketches, photostats of first selection, and final design, 11 x 8 ½ in. each
Subsequent to settling on a final design (after many sketches), SH drew this device on a computer screen, sending the final version to the Press on a disk. The photostats are exhibited by courtesy of the Press.

ABCD EFGHI JKLM NOPQ RSTUV XYZ &

The Electronic Scriptorium:
Two Cheers for Desktop Design

An Illustrated talk by Stephen Harvard on Wednesday, April 6, 1988 at the Club of Odd Volumes, 77 Mt. Vernon St. Social Hour at 5:30, Dinner at 6:30

The Society of Printers
For the Study and Advancement of the Art of Printing

Copenhaver Cumpston, President
Samuel Ellenport, Vice President
James R. Gill, Secretary
Marshall Henrichs, Treasurer
David L. Giele, Auditor
Council:
Albert Bachand, Melissa Clemence,
Richard Sheaff, Patricia Thoma

This notice was prepared by the speaker in a wood-heated farmhouse in Lost Nation, New Hampshire, six miles from the village. A Macintosh computer, Radius monitor, Abaton scanner, and a laser printer were the hardware; they perched, if not exactly on a desktop, then at least on a stout pine table. The alphabet on the cover and the two logos on this page were "drawn" electronically using Adobe Illustrator. This text was set in the italic of Sumner Stone's eponymous typeface; the makeup program was Quark Xpress. Text and graphics were output for final reproduction on a Linotronic 300 and printed by the Meriden-Stinehour Press in Lunenburg, Vermont.

The Printer & the Pardoner

Type Designs

38

Lower case roman "g", ca. 1981

Black ink and scraping on mylar, 5 ⅜ x 3 ⅜ in.

This drawing is for a proposed book typeface provisionally known as "Kestrel", which SH worked on for several years. The original commission to prepare drawings for this face, to be executed for photosetting, came in 1979 from the Merganthaler Company, which never released it. The design was later recommissioned by Adobe Systems, Inc., for digital typesetting, and SH began to adapt his earlier drawings during 1987 and 1988 (see below, Nos. 41–45).

39

"We are type designers . . ."

Offset lecture announcement, 5 x 6 in.

This quote by Rudolf Koch was designed by SH using his drawings for the italic version of his Kestrel typeface.

40

Lower case roman alphabet

Photostats mounted on a single sheet, 11 x 17 in.

41

Lower case roman "g", 1987

Computer printout, 11 x 8 ½ in.
Inscribed "6/22/87 10:44 AM"

This printout is one of many trials which were drawn on a screen using the Adobe Illustrator™ program.

42

Lower case roman "g", 1988

Computer printouts, each 11 x 8 ½ in., together 41 ½ x 31 ½ in.

An experiment in enlargement of the computer-drawn Kestrel type forms, which delighted the designer immensely.

43

"Verbs Go Human," 1987–88

Computer printout, 8 ½ x 11 in.
Inscribed "600 dpi [dots per inch]"

An experimental example of a text setting of Kestrel, to gauge its typeset appearance. This face was specifically designed to be for book texts, as explained by SH in a draft promotional statement: "Kestrel is a book type, designed for the sustained reading of scholarly and literary texts. . . . It is neither an historic revival nor a reworking of a twentieth century letterpress face. It is a digital type, intended to work because of, rather than in spite of, laser printers. . . . [It] carries in its design traces of the stonecutter's chisel, the scribe's reed pen, and the punchcutter's tempered burin: all of the tools that have shaped our evolving roman alphabet. . . . A book type can never rely on the playful invention possible in a commercial display face; it is beautiful only insofar as it is functional. It must be the Shaker chair among the overstuffed furniture of typography."

44

"Seashore," 1987–88

Computer printout, 11 x 8 ½ in.
Inscribed "600 dpi"

45

"Critique of Kestrel," 1987

Computer printout, 11 x 8 ½ in.
Dated "Fri Jul 17 13:09:54 PDT 1987"

One of a number of digital analyses of SH's drawings for Kestrel letters as they entered the design process at Adobe Systems, Inc.

GROLIER

ABC&DEFGHIJKLMNOPQRSTUVWXYZ

A NEW DISPLAY TYPE BY STEPHEN HARVARD FROM ADOBE SYSTEMS AND MERIDEN STINEHOUR

46

46

"Grolier—A New Display Type"

Computer printout, 8½ x 14 in.

Pursuing his devotion to the classic roman capitals, SH had designed a type alphabet which he christened "Grolier," from its first prominent use in *The Grolier Club 1884–1984 Its Library, Exhibitions, & Publications*, NY 1984 (see No. 14). He later transferred his models to a computer screen: "I'd like your comments on the enclosed caps, which I think are a good potential display type. The xerox is of an L-300 printout of my [Adobe] Illustrator™ art. This is a digitization of an alphabet I've used as an analogue cut-and-paste typeface for many years. It's a sixteenth-century cap (see enclosed Horfei xerox from Morison) with a monotype twist. It's *very* useful to me, since no photo type has these delicate proportions. I have, however, beefed up the serifs enough to survive, in the technical sense, output at text point sizes." (Letter to Sumner Stone, Adobe Systems, 17 Feb. 1988)

47

"Ravensong"

Computer printout, 8½ x 11 in.

This sample uses the Grolier capitals and an example of SH's computer-drawn illustrations.

48

"In the Beginning"

Computer printout, 11 x 8½ in.

49

Sketch for "Falstaff" Capitals

Graphite, 5⅝ x 5 in.

The alphabet dubbed "Falstaff" was intended as a bold version of Grolier, and this sketch sheet reveals various other possibilities for naming the face, including Rabelais, Pantagruel, and Firebird.

50

"Adams-Cataneo style Chancery Display"

Graphite, 11 x 8½ in.

These letters derive from the display lettering SH did for the 1979 Ansel Adams *Yosemite and the Range of Light* (see No. 11) and his own study of the Cataneo model book in the Houghton Library (see No. 64).

51

"Swash, Swashes, Formata 12°"

Graphite, 11 x 8½ in.

52

Monoweight Roman Display Capitals

Graphite, 8½ x 11 in.

This sans-serif capital is based in large part on classical inscriptions. The few samples shown here serve to indicate the wide range and great number of sketches and trials of different lettering styles in SH's files, many of which derived from handlettering which he had used in various design commissions.

SH AS STONECUTTER

53

ECL / EFL, 1973

Black slate, gilt, 6 x 7¼ in. (oval)
(Stone catalogue no. S16)
Lent by Mr. and Mrs. Edward Connery Lathem
"I have . . . given some thought to the decorative stone tablet which you proposed at our last meeting, and I enclose a rough sketch for your comments. In it you will see reflected my admiration for the early work of John Baskerville, whose stonecarving was as remarkable as his later punchcutting." (Letter to Edward Connery Lathem, 5 Aug. 1973)

54

Roman Capital Alphabet

Black slate, gilt, 13 x 23½ in.
(Stone catalogue no. S10)
Lent by Roderick Stinehour

55

Calligraphy, 1976

Green slate, ungilt, 8¾ x 11½ in.
(Stone catalogue no. S3)

56

Italic Alphabet

Black slate, gilt, 3⅞ x 12⅜ in.
(Stone catalogue no. S5)

57

Fulvous Harvest Mouse

Grey slate, gilt, 7½ x 5 in.
(Stone catalogue no. S2)

58

Arrangement of Ampersands, 1977

Black slate, gilt, 7¼ x 8¾ in. (oval)
(Stone catalogue no. S27)
Lent by Carolyn Coman & Lance Hidy
Described by the artist as "a flying passle of ampersands" (Letter to Carolyn Coman and Lance Hidy, 14 May 1977)

59

Roman Capital Alphabet, 1980

Black slate, gilt, 18 x 15 in.
(Stone catalogue no. S13)
Lent by David P. Becker

60

Roman Capital Alphabet, 1977

Black slate, gilt, 7⅜ x 6 in.
(Stone catalogue no. S6; study for the above stone)

61

Study for Inscriptional Letters, ca. 1979

Graphite, 9 x 7¼ in.
Drawing of sample letters preparatory to Archer gravestone (Stone catalogue no. S15).

RAVENSONG

47

SH AS AUTHOR

62

Ornamental Initials—The Woodcut Initials of Christopher Plantin—A Complete Catalogue
New York, The American Friends of the Plantin-Moretus Museum, 1974
12¼ x 9¼ in.
Begun by SH as a student project while abroad during his junior year at Dartmouth, this important publication appeared just four years after his graduation. He designed the entire text, handlettered the title-page plaque, and designed the decorative paper boards. Soon after seeing this book through the press, SH embarked on a catalogue of all of Christopher Plantin's botanical woodblocks—some 4,000 in all. The pressures of his other work prevented his completion of that project. (Writings catalogue no. W1)

63

Calligraphy for the Typographic Book, 1977
11 x 8 in.
Commissioned by the book arts journal *Fine Print*, this article served in many ways to introduce and highlight SH's work to a wider audience; a four-page centerfold with nineteen illustrations was the only selection of

his work published in his lifetime. He also designed the entire issue and lettered the masthead. (Writings catalogue no. W3)

64

An Italic Copybook—The Cataneo Manuscript

New York, Taplinger Publishing Company for The Department of Printing and Graphic Arts of the Houghton Library and The Newberry Library, 1981
8¾ x 10¼ in.

This project received its original impetus from Philip Hofer's encouraging SH to publish a book or manuscript in the collection of the Department of Printing and Graphic Arts. Upon discovering this manuscript, SH was immediately struck by its beauty, and conceived of this very striking facsimile joined with a scholarly examination of its style and importance. He designed the entire publication and hand-lettered the book-jacket titling. (Writings catalogue no. W9)

65

Alphabets of Grace, 1985

Letterpress wall calendar, 22 x 11 in.

This calligraphic and typographic calendar afforded SH an opportunity to explore varying displays of letters, alphabets, and text, while discussing the salient aspects of various letterforms in short explanations. Each page is a self-contained broadside. The trenchant quotations, culled from a large file in his studio, all have to do with the pleasures and arts of reading.

66

Prose Pieces, ca. 1985–88

Computer printouts, each 11 x 8½ in.

Revealing of a very private side and a deep, lifelong love of the natural world, these so-called "prose pieces" represent but two of over one hundred similar works (two complete pieces and fragments of others appear in the section of SH's writings on pp. 29–31). At the time of his death, SH was typesetting them on a computer, several in combination with computer-drawn illustrations. His files contain projected titles for the series, including "The Hillwind Meditations," "The Kitchen Broadsides," and "The Book of Ravensong." Other unpublished notes reveal the genesis of the form into which these pieces evolved: "What is a ravensong? A compressed utterance, a croak or squawk. Not smooth enough for poetry, not tame enough for prose. Ravensongs are outbursts. . . . It occurred to me that compression, a notable feature in the local geology, might also be a virtue in writing."

SH AS DRAFTSMAN & ILLUSTRATOR

67

Tree Stump

Wood engraving, 3 x 2 1/16 in.

A student work, this print was executed on the family farm of Paula McLain Harvard in Bremen, Maine.

67

The Mouse God

BY RICHARD KENNEDY

Pictures by Stephen Harvard

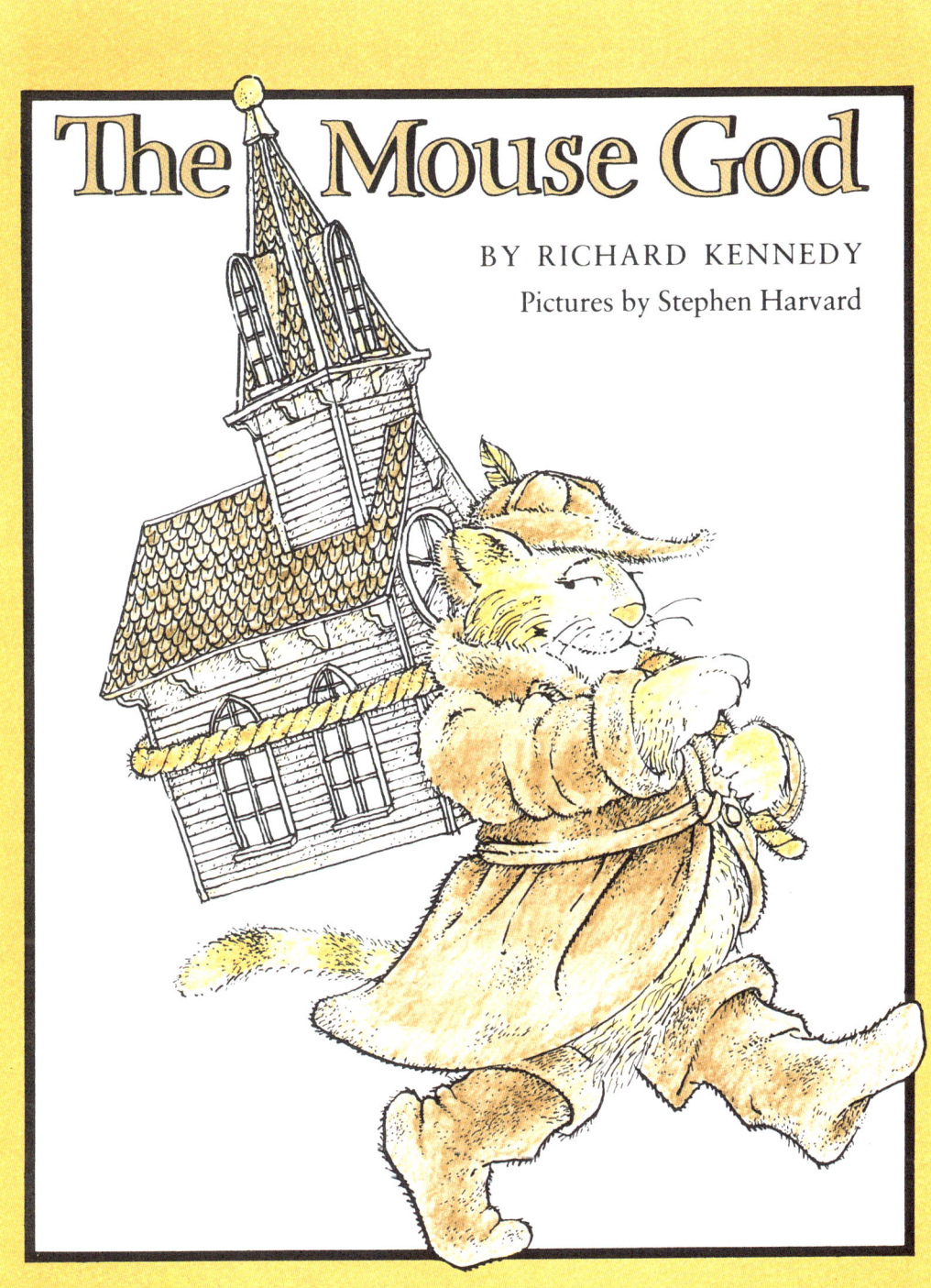

68

Portrait of Lance Hidy, ca. 1975–76

Graphite, 9 x 6 in.

As SH remarks in the accompanying letter, "Your studio must look something like this now—unless I've misrepresented the number of cats." (letter to Lance Hidy [n.d.].) Lent by Lance Hidy

69

Old MacBerlitz Had a Farm, from Noel Perrin, *First Person Rural* (Boston, David R. Godine, 1978), p. 107

Photo-offset illustration, 9 x 6 in. (page size)

Twelve full-page illustrations and two vignettes by SH accompany these humorous essays about living on a farm in Vermont.

70

Pig and Duck

Black ink and gouache drawing, 8 3/8 x 7 3/8 in.
Study for "Old MacBerlitz Had a Farm" (see No. 69).

71

Cat in a Mouse Coat, from Richard Kennedy, *The Mouse God* (Boston and Toronto, Little, Brown and Co., 1979)

Color photo-offset illustration, 9 1/4 x 7 3/4 in. (page size)

SH's only published illustrations for a children's book, these often full-page, carefully toned drawings were the object of special devotion and pride.

72

Cat in a Mouse Coat

Graphite, 10 1/16 x 7 in.
Study for the front cover illustration to *The Mouse God* (see No. 71).

73

St. Michael and the Dragon

Black ink, 4 5/8 x 6 1/4 in.
This drawing is one of several such "silhouetted" subjects included in this near-miniature sketchbook. The silhouette style was used particularly successfully in the endpaper illustrations to *The Mouse God* (see No. 71).

74

Child-creatures

Pen and black ink, 5 3/4 x 6 in.
Fanciful sketches of the artist's daughters when they were small children.

70

74

75

Decorative Initial (Leaf-Snout Beast)

Photostat of ink drawing, 11 x 8½ in.
Drawing in photostat form used to decorate numerous missives to friends.
Lent by Lance Hidy

76

Whitethroat Sparrow on u Mossy Branch
Early 1980s

Gouache, 11½ x 14½ in.
Signed in graphite lower right "Harvard"
The natural world was a constant source of inspiration, and there are dozens of drawings and sketches of birds, animals, and plants in the artist's archives.

75

76

77
Study of a Plant
Brown ink and wash over graphite, 13 x 9⅞ in.

78
Leaf Forms, ca. 1987
Graphite, 11 x 8½ in.

79
Leaf Forms, 1987
Computer-drawn printout, 11 x 8½ in.
Having scanned the above pencil sketch onto the computer screen, SH manipulated the image and drew further enhancements to produce this image, one of a large number of similar leaf designs intended to illustrate a never-executed printing of a poem by Sappho.

79

Published Writings

NOTE: The following listing includes all published writings of Stephen Harvard located by the compiler, arranged in chronological order by date of publication. Each work has been given a number preceded by "W". Reviews by other writers of two publications (W1 and W9) are also included. The Farrell citations refer to the checklist in David Farrell, *The Stinehour Press, A Bibliographical Checklist of the First Thirty Years*, Lunenburg, Meriden-Stinehour Press, 1988.

W1

Ornamental Initials: The Woodcut Initials of Christopher Plantin. A Complete Catalogue, New York, The American Friends of the Plantin-Moretus Museum, 1974. Farrell 648.
Also designed by SH, including title page lettering and endpapers.
Reviews: John Dreyfus, in *Times Literary Supplement*, 29 Nov 1974; Elly Cockx-Indestege, in *Quaerendo*, vol. 5, no. 1 (1975), pp. 76–77; Nicolas Barker, in *The Book Collector* (Summer 1976), pp. 261–66; Helmut Urban, in *Gutenberg-Jahrbuch 1978*, p. 263.

W2

A Printer's Emblems, [Lunenburg, The Stinehour Press] 1976. Farrell 788.

W3

"Calligraphy for the Typographic Book," *Fine Print*, vol. 3, no. 3 (July 1977), pp. 1–4.
The title lettering and design of entire issue also by SH; includes a four-page centerfold with reproductions of his designs.

W4

Review of three books printed by The Perishable Press Limited, Mount Horeb, Wisconsin. *Fine Print*, vol. 3, no. 4 (Oct. 1977), pp. 84–86.

W5

Review of Reynolds Stone, *Reynolds Stone Engravings*. *Fine Print*, vol. 4, no. 3 (July 1978), pp. 83–84.

W6

Review of Frank J. Anderson, *Private Presswork: A Bibliographic Approach to Printing as an Avocation*. *Fine Print*, vol. 4, no. 4 (Oct. 1978), p. 116.

W7
Vision & Revision: Introducing Meriden-Stinehour Incorporated, Meriden [CT] and Lunenburg [VT], Meriden-Stinehour, Inc., 1979. Farrell 1002.
Captions under the photographs by SH.

W8
Review of James Moran, *Heraldic Influence on Early Printers' Devices. Fine Print*, vol. 5, no. 3 (July 1979), pp. 88–91.

W9
An Italic Copybook – The Cataneo Manuscript, New York, Taplinger Publishing Company, for the Department of Printing and Graphic Arts of the Houghton Library, Harvard University, and The Newberry Library, 1981. Fifth in the series of *Studies in the History of Calligraphy*.
Book-jacket calligraphy and entire design by SH.
Reviewed by: R. Williams, in *Fine Print*, vol. 8, no. 4 (Oct 1982), pp. 145, 153–54; Sheila Waters, in *Scripsit* [Journal of the Washington Calligraphy Guild], (Dec 1982), pp. 16–17 [reprinted elsewhere]; Sheila Waters, in *Printing History*, vol. 6, no. 2 (1984), pp. 36–38. [Also James Hayes, in a never-published trial issue of *Typographia I* (1982), pp. 45–47].

W10
Review of A. S. Osley, *Scribes and Sources: Handbook of the Chancery Hand in the Sixteenth Century. Fine Print*, vol. 7, no. 1 (Jan 1981), pp. 26–29.

W11
"Champ Fleury by Geofroy Tory", *BR Today: A Selection of his Books with Comments*, New York, The Grolier Club, 1982, p. 18.

W12
Alphabets of Grace – A Calendar of Letterforms & Type Designs, Dobbs Ferry [NY], Cahill & Company [1985].
SH designed several of the alphabets and the layout, selected quotations from writers, and wrote comments on typefaces and letterforms.

W13
"Jury Comments", *The 1985 New England Book Show* [sponsored by Bookbuilders of Boston, n.p., n.d.], pp. 20–21.

W14
"The Long Making", *Ray Nash and the Graphic Arts Workshop at Dartmouth College*, Hanover [NH], The Friends of the Dartmouth Library, 1987, pp. 69–73.
The lettering on the title page is also by SH.

W15
"Ray Nash", *Proceedings of the American Antiquarian Society*, vol. 97, pt. 1 (1987), pp. 29–32.

W16
"Notes on developing a logo", reproduced in an article, "More on Stephen Harvard's Program". *Connecticut Valley Calligraphers Newsletter*, vol. 4, no. 3 (Feb. 1988), p. 9.

W17
A Toast in Absentia, 4 July 1988.
Broadside printed in honor of Sandra Kirshenbaum's fiftieth birthday by the Meriden-Stinehour Press, 1988. The design and monogram are also by SH.

W18
"Even the Smallest Drawing", *Printing History*, vol. 10, no. 2 (1988), p. 3.

W19
"The Book of Strategy", *The Mirror*, vol. 1, no. 1 (Fall 1989), p. 3.

Catalogue of Inscriptional Stonework

NOTE: This listing includes all inscriptional stones by Stephen Harvard located by the compiler, arranged by ownership and/or present location. Measurements are height before width. Each work has been given a number preceded by "S". Information concerning additional stones is welcome.

PAULA HARVARD · Lancaster, New Hampshire

S1
By Hammer and Hand All Works Do Stand
Black slate, ungilt
10 ⅛ x 17 ⅞ in.
Paula Harvard indicates this is an early work.

S2
Relief carving of a Harvest Mouse
"Reithrodontomys fulvescens"
Grey slate, gilt
7 ½ x 5 in.

S3
Calligraphy, 1976
Green slate, ungilt
8 ¾ x 11 ½ in.
Signed verso: "Stephen Harvard / 1976"

S4
Relief carving of a Flower
"CINQVEFOIL Potentilla Procumbens Rosaceae"
Purple slate, ungilt
18 x 13 in.

S5
Italic Alphabet
Black slate, gilt
3 ⅞ x 12 ⅜ in.

S6
Roman Alphabet, 1977
Black slate, gilt
7 ⅜ x 6 in.
Signed verso: "Stephen Harvard 1977"
Study for Becker alphabet stone (see cat. S13).

S7
Relief carving of a Ram
Indiana limestone
14 ½ x 14 ½ in. (irregular)

S8
Italic Alphabet
Black slate, ungilt
11 ½ x 11 ½ in.

SHELAGH HARVARD · Lancaster, New Hampshire

S9
Relief carving of Owl and Pussycat
Soapstone
7 ¾ x 10 in.
Verso: initials "SMH" [Shelagh Mountain Harvard]

ELIZABETH & RODERICK STINEHOUR
Lunenburg, Vermont

S10
Roman Alphabet

Black slate, gilt
13 x 23 ½ in.

S11
Peter Stinehour Memorial
"PETER DOUGLAS / 4 NOVEMBER 1957 / 12 APRIL 1975"
Black slate, ungilt
9 x 19 in.
This stone was executed as a memorial headstone for the owners' son, but was never installed. Stephen did eventually design the lettering for the granite stones for the Stinehour family in the Lancaster, NH, cemetery, which was executed commercially.

NANCY SOUTHWORTH · Lancaster, New Hampshire

S12
Relief carving of a Sunburst
"NS"
Soapstone
9 ½ x 6 in.

DAVID P. BECKER · Boston, Massachusetts

S13
Roman Alphabet
Black slate, gilt
18 x 15 in.
See cat. S6 for the study for this stone.

NANCY HUGO · New Canaan, Connecticut

S14
Italic Alphabet
Black slate, gilt
10 x 16 ½ in.
Commissioned by E. Harold Hugo.

WILLIAMS COLLEGE CEMETERY
Williamstown, Massachusetts

S15
Archer Headstone
"H. RICHARD / ARCHER / 1911 – 1978 / Chapin Librarian / MARGOT HANKO / ARCHER"
Green slate, letters highlighted with pigment
41 ½ x 24 in.

ELIZABETH & EDWARD CONNERY LATHEM
Hanover, New Hampshire

S16
Lathem Duogram, 1973
"ECL / EFL"
Black slate, gilt
6 x 7 ¼ in. (oval)
See *Fine Print*, vol. 3, no. 3 (July 1977), p. 51, no. 10, and p. 63, fig. 10, for a reproduction of this design.

DARTMOUTH COLLEGE CEMETERY
Hanover, New Hampshire

S17
Dickerson Headstone
"ALBERT INSKIP / DICKERSON / 1908 – 1972 / Dean of Freshmen / Dartmouth College / His Wife / LUCIA WEIMER / DICKERSON / 1907 – "
Verso: "[carving of branch with three apples] / DICKERSON"
Black slate, ungilt
39 x 24 in.

DARTMOUTH COLLEGE LIBRARY
Hanover, New Hampshire

S18
Woodward Room, 1973
"This room, containing the surviving books / of the earliest Library of Dartmouth / College, is equipped in

memory of / BEZALEEL WOODWARD, A.M. / a Tutor, Treasurer, Trustee and / Vice-President of the College; its first / Librarian and its first professor of Mathematics and Natural Philosophy / ET HIS PRIN-CIPIIS VIA / STERNITVR AD MAIORA"
Black slate, gilt
17 x 12 ½ in.

S19
Larmon Room, 1974
"This room in memory of / RUSSELL 'COTTY' LARMON / Class of 1919 / teacher and administrator / has been established by / his classmates and friends / 1974"
Black slate, gilt
14 ½ x 14 in.

S20
Class of 1926 Room
"This room is a memorial to / THE CLASS OF 1926"
Black slate, gilt
3 ½ x 8 in.

S21
Jones Microtext Center, 1975
"JONES MICROTEXT CENTER / established in memory of / BERKELEY FAIRFAX JONES / Class of 1925 / by his family and friends"
Black slate with platinum
13 x 15 ½ in.

S22
Truxal Room, 1976
"This room is a memorial to / ANDREW G. TRUXAL"
Black slate, gilt
3 ⅞ x 12 in.

S23
The Hicks Room, 1978
"The HICKS Room"
Black slate, gilt
4 x 12 in.

S24
The Lathem Room, 1978
"The LATHEM Room"
Black slate, gilt
4 x 12 in.

S25
The Lathem Room, 1978
"This room honors / EDWARD / CONNERY / LATHEM / CLASS OF 1951 / fifteenth Librarian of the / College and first Dean / of Libraries"
Black slate, gilt
24 x 20 in. (oval)

S26
The Manley Room, 1984
"The LOUISE H. MANLEY Room"
Black slate, gilt
3 x 15 ¼ in.

CAROLYN COMAN & LANCE HIDY
Newburyport, Massachusetts

S27
Arrangement of Ampersands, 1977
Black slate, gilt
7 ¼ x 8 ¾ in. (oval)
Signed verso: "S Harvard 77"
This and the following stone were wedding presents.

DAVID R. GODINE · Boston, Massachusetts

S28
Ampersand
Brown slate, gilt
4 ⅞ x 5 ⅞ in.

BOSTON PUBLIC LIBRARY
Boston, Massachusetts

S29
The McCord Study, 1979
"THE / David McCord / STUDY"
Black slate, gilt
10½ x 17 in.

PRINCETON UNIVERSITY LIBRARY
Princeton, New Jersey

S30
The Hamilton Room, ca. 1980
"THE SINCLAIR HAMILTON / CLASS OF 1906 / COLLECTION OF AMERICAN / ILLUSTRATED BOOKS"
Black slate, gilt
12 x 36 in.

JOLENE UNSOELD · Olympia, Washington

S31
Nanda Devi Unsoeld Memorial
"NANDA DEVI / SEPTEMBER 8, 1976 / NANDA DEVI / The mountain and I, / We never grow tired of each other"
Black slate, gilt
Commissioned as a memorial by the parents of Nanda Devi Unsoeld, who died while climbing the mountain in the Himalayan range which was her namesake.

PINE KNOLL CEMETERY · Hanover, New Hampshire

S32
Nash Headstone
"RAY NASH / 1905–1982 / AND HIS WIFE / HOPE / 1907– "
Green slate
36 x 24 in.

WEEKS MEMORIAL HOSPITAL
Lancaster, New Hampshire

S33
Weeks Hospital Entrance Hall, 1976
"It is the wish of the trustees to give grateful / recognition to the living descendants of Philip / Sidney Rust of South Paris, Maine, and Irénée / du Pont of Wilmington, Delaware, for their past / and continuing aid to the needs of the Beatrice / D. Weeks Memorial Hospital. 1976"
Black slate, gilt
18 x 24 in.

S34
Wemyss Dining Facility, 1976
"IN GRATEFUL APPRECIATION / TO JAMES C. WEMYSS, SR. / JAMES C. WEMYSS, JR. & FAMILY / FOR THIS KITCHEN AND / DINING FACILITY 1976."
Black slate, gilt
18 x 24 in.

ST. JOHNSBURY ACADEMY
St. Johnsbury, Vermont

S35
Farmer Memorial
"IN MEMORY OF / HOWARD J. FARMER, M.D. / CLASS OF 1928 / MEMBER, BOARD OF TRUSTEES / 1949–1973 / PRESIDENT OF THE BOARD / 1951–1973"
Green slate, gilt
23 x 30 in.

LOCATION UNKNOWN

S36
Powers Headstone
"*Susan Moore Powers* / 1908–1974"
A photograph of SH cutting this stone is in the collection of Paula Harvard (see opposite).

THE WORK OF STEPHEN HARVARD

*has been composed, printed, and bound by
Meriden-Stinehour Press. The text type is Palatino with
Diotima for display. The papers used are Mohawk Superfine
text and Curtis Tweedweave Duplex cover stock.
An edition of two thousand copies was produced
in March 1990 in Lunenburg, Vermont.
Design by Christopher Kuntze*